Volume **1**

Music for Millions

World Famous

PIANO
PIECES

Edited by Hugo Frey

ISBN 0-8256-4001-6

Consolidated Music Publishers, Inc., 33 West 60th Street, New York 10023

Price: $3.95 MSC

Contents by Titles

Contents by Composers

EMPEROR WALTZ

JOHANN STRAUSS

CONCERTO
Op. 18—THEMES

Transcription by
Hugo Frey

SERGEI RACHMANINOFF

(2nd Theme)
Moderately slow

POLONAISE

Op. 53—THEME

*Arranged by
Hugo Frey*

FREDERIC CHOPIN

Maestoso

PETER AND THE WOLF

Arranged by
Hugo Frey   Slow march tempo

SERGEI PROKOFIEFF

CONCERTO

Op. 16—THEMES

Arranged by
Hugo Frey

EDVARD GRIEG

Allegro, molto moderato

CONCERTO
Op. 23—THEME

Arranged by
Hugo Frey

PETER TSCHAIKOWSKY

LIEBESTRAUM

Arranged by
Hugo Frey

FRANZ LISZT

Very slow and with expression

SIXTH SYMPHONY

THEME

Arranged by
Hugo Frey

PETER TSCHAIKOWSKY

Andantino

CONCERTO
Op. 54—THEME

Arranged by
Hugo Frey

ROBERT SCHUMANN

TANGO IN D

Arranged by
Hugo Frey

ISAAC ALBENIZ

Moderate Tango tempo

UNFINISHED SYMPHONY

THEME

*Arranged by
Hugo Frey*

FRANZ SCHUBERT

REVERIE

*Arranged by
Hugo Frey*

CLAUDE DEBUSSY

Andantino espressivo

28

COUNTRY GARDENS

Arranged by
Hugo Frey

TRADITIONAL

Moderately bright tempo

POEM

ZDENKO FIBICH

Slowly, with expression

SERENADE

Arranged by
Hugo Frey

VICTOR HERBERT

Andantino grazioso

33

THIRD SYMPHONY

ALLEGRETTO

*Arranged by
D. Savino*

JOHANNES BRAHMS

Allegretto

FINLANDIA

Arranged by
Hugo Frey

JAN SIBELIUS

Moderately bright (*slow two beats*)

KREUTZER SONATA

THEME

Arranged by
Hugo Frey

LUDWIG VAN BEETHOVEN

VIENNESE REFRAIN

*Arranged by
Hugo Frey*

TRADITIONAL

Slow with expression

CANZONETTA

Arranged by
Hugo Frey

VICTOR HERBERT

Allegretto

Try for 66

THE SWAN

Arranged by
Hugo Frey

CAMILLE SAINT-SAËNS

Slowly, with expression

p (with pedal)

Danube Waves

Introduction
Allegro moderato

JAN IVANOVICI

CONSOLIDATED MUSIC PUBLISHERS, INC., New York, N. Y.

Fine

D.S. al Fine

Coda

LULLABY

JOHANNES BRAHMS

SONGS MY MOTHER TAUGHT ME

Slowly, with expression

ANTON DVORAK

CONSOLIDATED MUSIC PUBLISHERS, INC., New York, N. Y.

THE YOUNG PRINCE AND THE YOUNG PRINCESS

from "SCHEHEREZADE"

NICOLAS RIMSKY-KORSAKOFF

Andantino, quasi allegretto M.M. ♩. = 54

HUMORESQUE

ANTON DVORAK

Poco Lento e grazioso. M.M. ♩=72.

CONSOLIDATED MUSIC PUBLISHERS, INC., New York, N. Y.

52

BALLET MUSIC

from "ROSAMUNDE"

FRANZ SCHUBERT

CONSOLIDATED MUSIC PUBLISHERS, INC., New York, N. Y.

STRAUSS WALTZ MEDLEY

JOHANN STRAUSS

TALES FROM THE VIENNA WOODS

CONSOLIDATED MUSIC PUBLISHERS, INC., New York, N. Y.

Fine

D.S. al Fine

ON THE BEAUTIFUL BLUE DANUBE

CHANSON TRISTE

Op. 40—No. 2

PETER TSCHAIKOWSKY

Allegro non troppo
la melodia molto espress.

CONSOLIDATED MUSIC PUBLISHERS, INC., New York, N. Y.

IL BACIO

LUIGI ARDITI

Tempo di Valse

CONSOLIDATED MUSIC PUBLISHERS, INC., New York, N. Y.

MAZURKA

Op. 24—No. 3

FREDERIC CHOPIN

CONSOLIDATED MUSIC PUBLISHERS, INC., New York, N. Y.

PIZZICATI

from "SYLVIA"

LEO DELIBES

CONSOLIDATED MUSIC PUBLISHERS, INC., New York, N. Y.

66

MINUET

from "DON JUAN"

WOLFGANG MOZART

Moderato

CONSOLIDATED MUSIC PUBLISHERS, INC., New York, N. Y.

SEMPER FIDELIS

MARCH

JOHN PHILIP SOUSA

CONSOLIDATED MUSIC PUBLISHERS, INC., New York, N. Y.

MORNING

from "PEER GYNT"

EDVARD GRIEG

Allegretto pastorale. ♩. = 60.

CONSOLIDATED MUSIC PUBLISHERS, INC., New York, N. Y.

BERCEUSE

from "JOCELYN"

BENJAMIN GODARD

CONSOLIDATED MUSIC PUBLISHERS, INC., New York, N. Y.

PRELUDE

Op. 28—No. 7

FREDERIC CHOPIN

PRELUDE

Op. 28—No. 20

FREDERIC CHOPIN

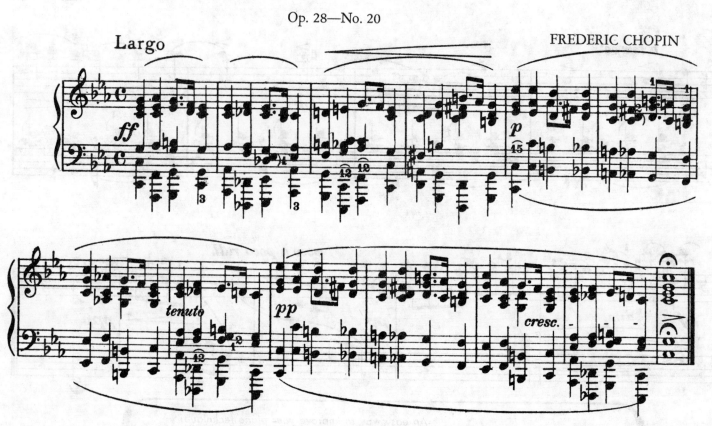

CONSOLIDATED MUSIC PUBLISHERS, INC., New York, N. Y.

WALTZ

Op. 39—No. 15

JOHANNES BRAHMS

CONSOLIDATED MUSIC PUBLISHERS, INC., New York, N. Y.

SERENADE BADINE

GABRIEL MARIE

Scherzando

CONSOLIDATED MUSIC PUBLISHERS, INC., New York, N. Y.

SECOND SYMPHONY

THEME

JOHANNES BRAHMS

CONSOLIDATED MUSIC PUBLISHERS, INC., New York, N. Y.

MOONLIGHT SONATA

THEME

LUDWIG VAN BEETHOVEN

Adagio sostenuto

86

ROMANCE

Op. 44—No. 1

ANTON RUBINSTEIN

CONSOLIDATED MUSIC PUBLISHERS, INC., New York, N. Y.

SERENADE

FRANZ SCHUBERT

CONSOLIDATED MUSIC PUBLISHERS, INC., New York, N. Y.

MEPHISTO WALTZ

THEME

FRANZ LISZT

CONSOLIDATED MUSIC PUBLISHERS, INC., New York, N. Y.

TAMBOURIN

G. F. RAMEAU

CONSOLIDATED MUSIC PUBLISHERS, INC., New York, N. Y.

MOMENT MUSICALE

Op. 94—No. 3

FRANZ SCHUBERT

Allegro moderato (♩=92)

CONSOLIDATED MUSIC PUBLISHERS, INC., New York, N. Y.

LARGO

G. F. HANDEL

Very slow (*with feeling*)

CONSOLIDATED MUSIC PUBLISHERS, INC., New York, N. Y.

THE WASHINGTON POST

MARCH

JOHN PHILIP SOUSA

Tempo marziale.

CONSOLIDATED MUSIC PUBLISHERS, INC., New York, N. Y.

CHACONNE

AUGUSTE DURAND

CONSOLIDATED MUSIC PUBLISHERS, INC., New York, N. Y.

105

AMARYLLIS

Allegro moderato

HENRI GHYS

CONSOLIDATED MUSIC PUBLISHERS, INC., New York, N. Y.

(Very delicate)

MINUTE WALTZ

Op. 64—No. 1

Molto vivace.
leggiero

FREDERIC CHOPIN

CONSOLIDATED MUSIC PUBLISHERS, INC., New York, N. Y.

TRAUMEREI

ROBERT SCHUMANN

CONSOLIDATED MUSIC PUBLISHERS, INC., New York, N. Y.

ANITRA'S DANCE

from "PEER GYNT"

EDVARD GRIEG

Tempo di Mazurka. ♩ = 160.

114

PRELUDE AND FUGUE IN C

from "WELL TEMPERED CLAVICHORD"

J. S. BACH

PRELUDE
Allegro.

CONSOLIDATED MUSIC PUBLISHERS, INC., New York, N. Y.

FUGUE
Four Voices

Moderato

SONG WITHOUT WORDS

Op. 2—No. 3

PETER TSCHAIKOWSKY

Allegretto grazioso e cantabile

I. Tempo

PRELUDE IN C# MINOR

SERGEI RACHMANINOFF

CONSOLIDATED MUSIC PUBLISHERS, INC., New York, N. Y.

ALLA TURCA

WOLFGANG MOZART

CONSOLIDATED MUSIC PUBLISHERS, INC., New York, N. Y.

MINUET

L. BOCCHERINI

Moderato

CONSOLIDATED MUSIC PUBLISHERS, INC., New York, N. Y.

TRIO

POLKA

from "L'AGE d'OR"

DMITRI SHOSTAKOVITCH

Allegretto

CONSOLIDATED MUSIC PUBLISHERS, INC., New York, N. Y.

TWO GUITARS

Arranged by
Hugo Frey

TRADITIONAL

CONSOLIDATED MUSIC PUBLISHERS, INC., New York, N. Y.

Moderately fast tempo

Moderately bright tempo

MINUET

from Op. 78

FRANZ SCHUBERT

Allegro moderato ♩ = 168

CONSOLIDATED MUSIC PUBLISHERS, INC., New York, N. Y.

Minuet D. C.

PAVANE

Arranged by
Hugo Frey

MAURICE RAVEL

STAR OF THE SEA

Moderato

AMANDA KENNEDY

CONSOLIDATED MUSIC PUBLISHERS, INC., New York, N. Y.

ALLEGRETTO

from "SEVENTH SYMPHONY"

LUDWIG VAN BEETHOVEN

CONSOLIDATED MUSIC PUBLISHERS, INC., New York, N. Y.

HUNGARIAN DANCE

No. 5

JOHANNES BRAHMS

CONSOLIDATED MUSIC PUBLISHERS, INC., New York, N. Y.

146

MINUET IN G

LUDWIG VAN BEETHOVEN

Allegretto

CONSOLIDATED MUSIC PUBLISHERS, INC., New York, N. Y.

NOCTURNE

Op. 9—No. 2

FREDERIC CHOPIN

CONSOLIDATED MUSIC PUBLISHERS, INC., New York, N. Y.

SPRING SONG

Allegretto grazioso

FELIX MENDELSSOHN

CONSOLIDATED MUSIC PUBLISHERS, INC., New York, N. Y.

ALLEGRETTO

from QUARTET No. 34

F. J. HAYDN

Allegretto scherzando ♩ = 126

CONSOLIDATED MUSIC PUBLISHERS, INC., New York, N. Y.

THE HAPPY FARMER

ROBERT SCHUMANN

CONSOLIDATED MUSIC PUBLISHERS, INC., New York, N. Y.

LA PALOMA

SEBASTIAN YRADIER

Allegro moderato

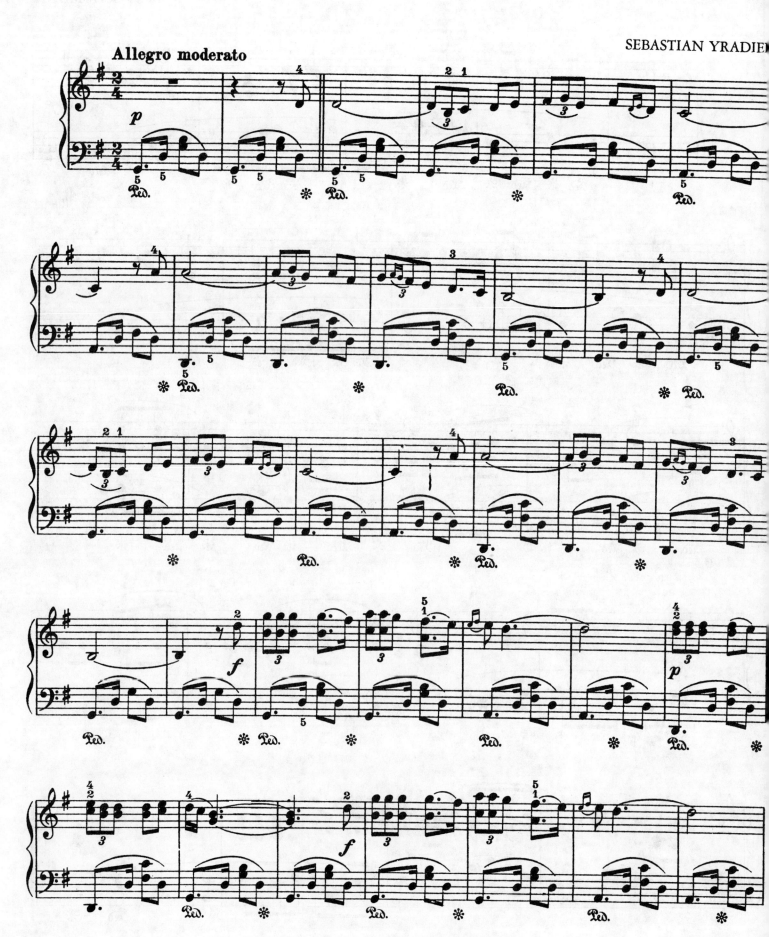

CONSOLIDATED MUSIC PUBLISHERS, INC., New York, N. Y.

BRIDAL CHORUS

from "LOHENGRIN"

RICHARD WAGNER

WEDDING MARCH

FELIX MENDELSSOHN

CONSOLIDATED MUSIC PUBLISHERS, INC., New York, N. Y.

VOLGA BOAT SONG

Arranged by
Hugo Frey

TRADITIONAL